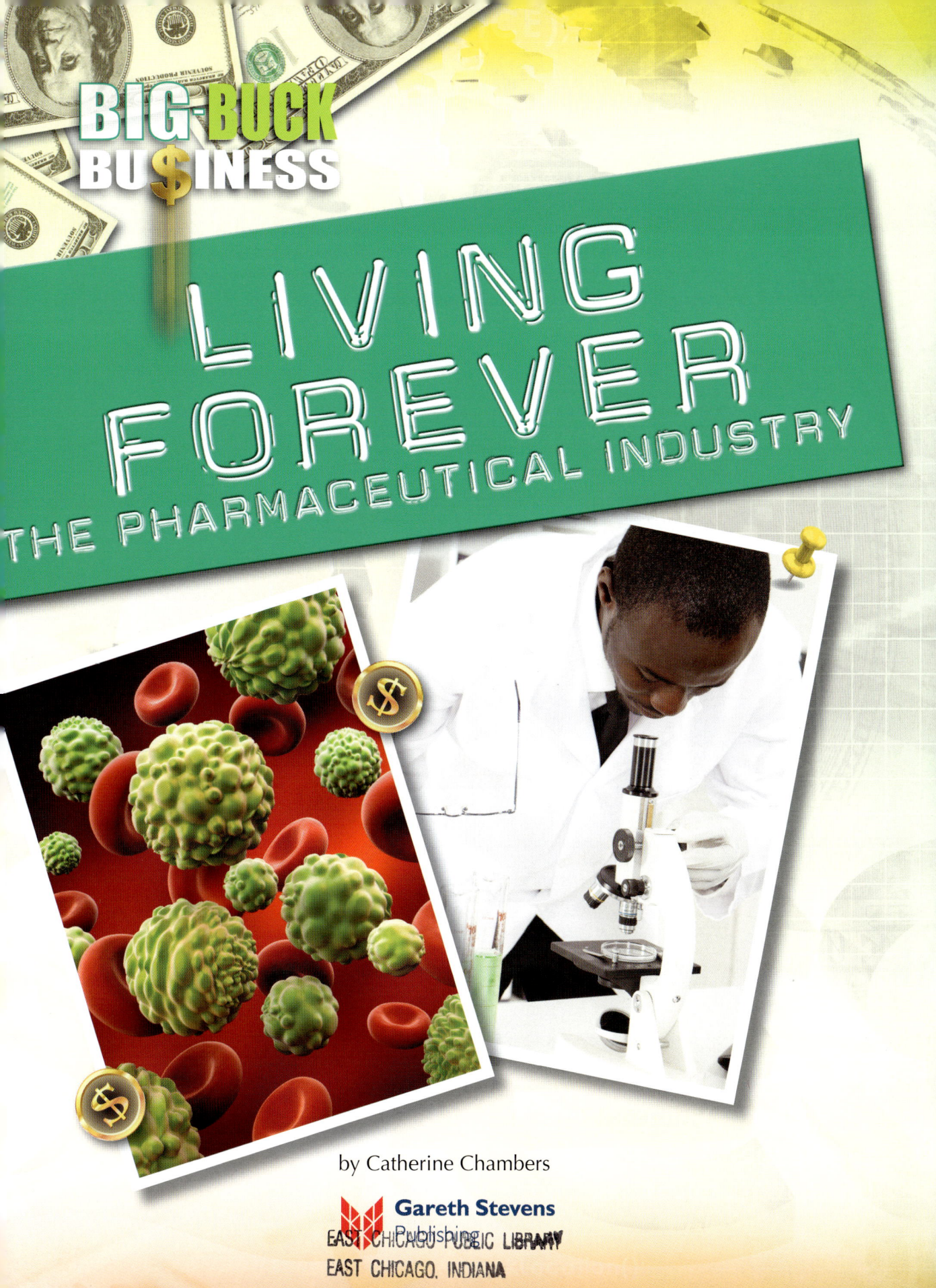

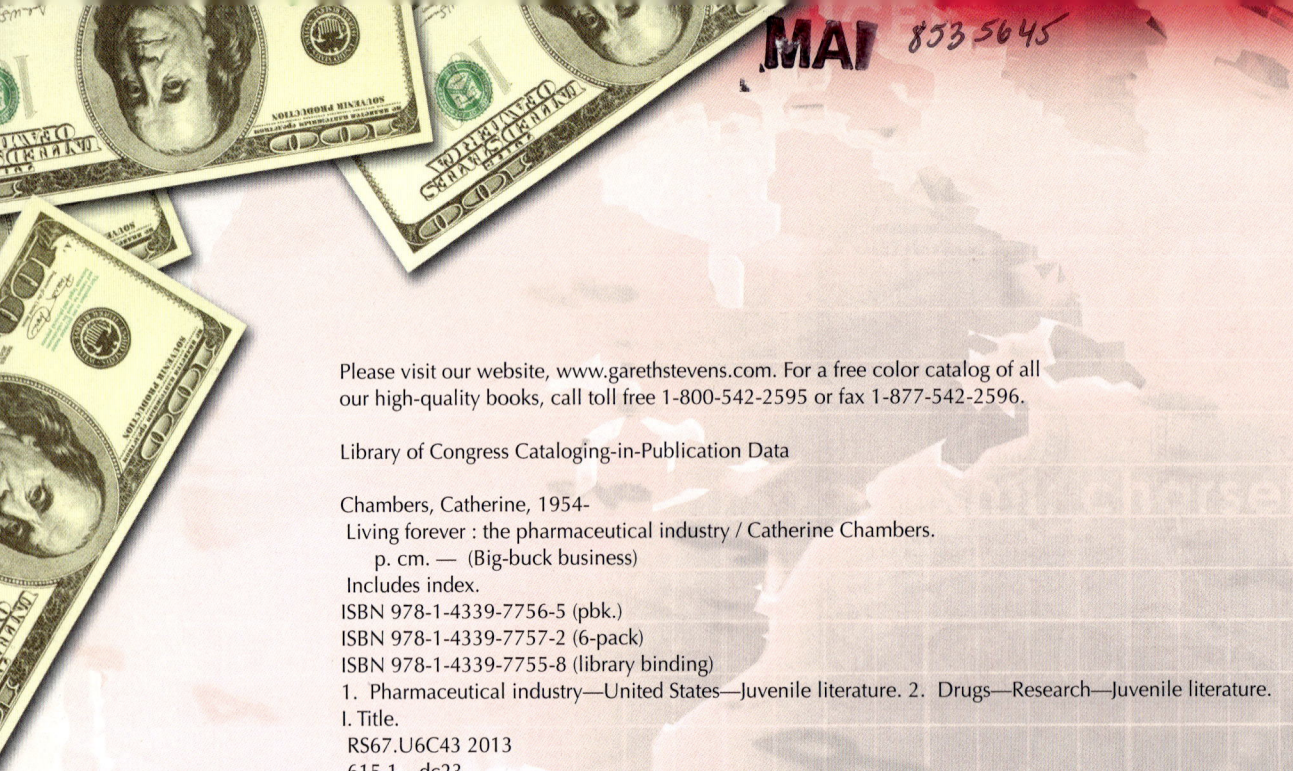

Please visit our website, www.garethstevens.com. For a free color catalog of all our high-quality books, call toll free 1-800-542-2595 or fax 1-877-542-2596.

Library of Congress Cataloging-in-Publication Data

Chambers, Catherine, 1954-
 Living forever : the pharmaceutical industry / Catherine Chambers.
     p. cm. — (Big-buck business)
 Includes index.
 ISBN 978-1-4339-7756-5 (pbk.)
 ISBN 978-1-4339-7757-2 (6-pack)
 ISBN 978-1-4339-7755-8 (library binding)
 1. Pharmaceutical industry—United States—Juvenile literature. 2. Drugs—Research—Juvenile literature. I. Title.
 RS67.U6C43 2013
 615.1—dc23
                                        2012006406

First Edition

Published in 2013 by
Gareth Stevens Publishing
111 East 14th Street, Suite 349
New York, NY 10003

© 2013 Gareth Stevens Publishing

Produced by Calcium Creative Ltd
Designed by Nick Leggett
Edited by Sarah Eason and Vicky Egan
Picture research by Susannah Jayes

Photo credits: Cover: Shutterstock: Kayros Studio l, Nenov Brothers Photography r. Inside: Dreamstime: Alexskopje 36bl, Radu Razvan Gheorghe 41b, Huating 10tr, Samrar35 27t, Tbe 21cl; Istockphoto: Ana Abejon 31t, Nazvin Alexey 17br, Darren Baker 5tr, Michele Galli 34, Jodi Jacobson 16bc, Kali9 44tr, Mangostock 4–5, Monkey Business Images 42b, Neustockimages 18bl Baris Simsek 1l, 25tr, Roel Smart 8br, YinYang 23t; David Jordan 33cl; Library of Congress: 7b; National Library of Medicine: 9t; Shutterstock: Anyaivanova 13b, Yuri Arcurs 11t, 25bl, 28br, 35tr, Roxana Bashyrova 3cr, Diego Cervo 30cl, P Cruciatti 6bl, Ermek 22b, Iofoto 19b, Michael Jung 1r, Ragne Kabanova 14r, Kheng Guan Toh 40bl, Robert Kneschke 43tr, Rob Marmion 38br, Mikeledray 16–17, Monkey Business Images 26b, Nico Tucol 20–21, Picsfive 29tl, Poznyakov 45tr, Sgame 39t, AISPIX by Image Source 32b, Thefinalmiracle 37br, Ints Vikmanis 16br, Vovan 44br, Wavebreakmedia ltd 15b; Wikipedia: 12bl.

All rights reserved. No part of this book may be reproduced in any form without permission from the publisher, except by reviewer.

Printed in the United States of America

CPSIA compliance information: Batch #CS12GS: For further information contact Gareth Stevens, New York, New York at 1-800-542-2595.

Introduction: Medicines Without Frontiers	4
Chapter 1: Rise of the Pharmaceutical Industry	6
Medical Wonders	8
Chapter 2: Making Medicines	10
Research and Development	12
Clinical Trials	14
Patent Pending	16
Marketing Medicines	18
Chapter 3: The Big Players	20
Risky Business	22
Billion-Dollar Businesses	24
Managing the Image	26
Chapter 4: Controversies and Challenges	28
Fear Tactics?	30
The Cost of Error	32
Cozy Relationships	34
Global Issues	36
Chapter 5: Future of Pharmaceuticals	38
Age of the Internet	40
Fighting Illegal Medicines	42
Conclusion: Living Forever	44
Glossary	46
For More Information	47
Index	48

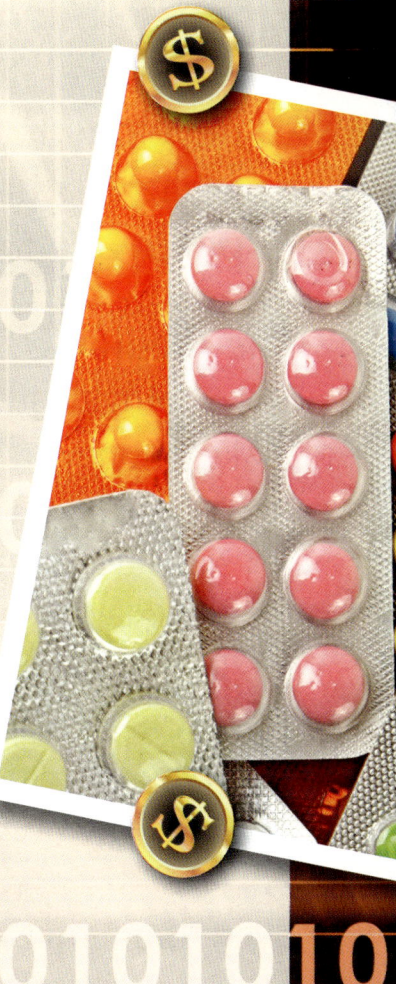

MEDICINES WITHOUT FRONTIERS

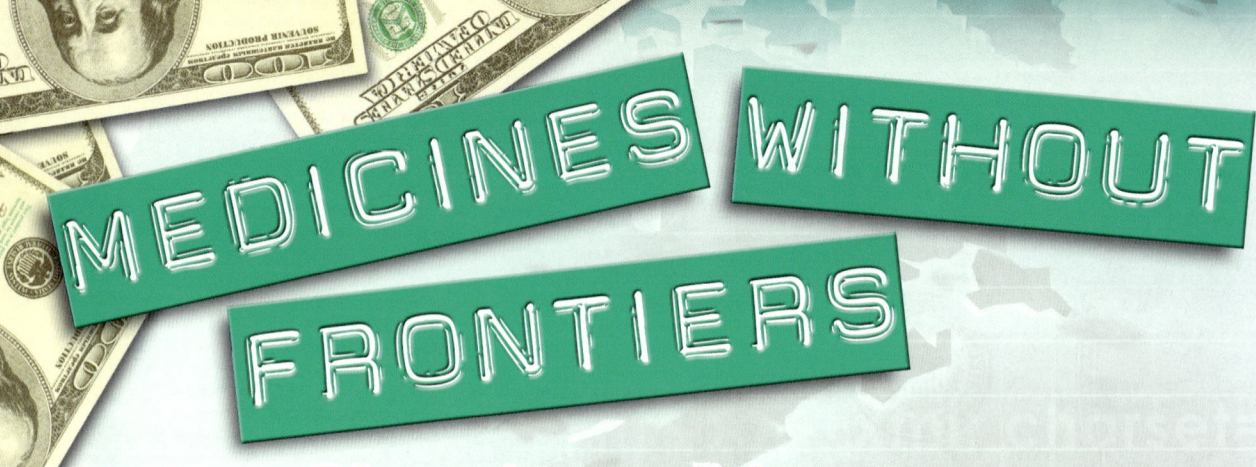

We have all been given medicines that have helped us get well when we've been sick. Have you ever wondered, though, who discovered, developed, and manufactured these amazing cures? The answer is the pharmaceutical industry.

Every time you go to a drugstore to buy medicine, you are helping the pharmaceutical industry grow.

The medicine business

The pharmaceutical industry makes money by making and selling medicines. Because people get sick all the time, there is a huge demand for their products. In 2008 alone, the world's top 20 pharmaceutical corporations sold over $500 million worth of drugs. One leading company, Pfizer, announced profits of over $8 billion that year. The business of medicine makes a great deal of money.

A healthy future

Making medicines is a complicated task. It can take many years to produce a new drug and prove that it is safe to use. The industry employs about 1.5 million people worldwide, and that figure is set to rise. As we all live longer, the need for medicines will increase. The pharmaceutical industry will be announcing record profits for years to come.

Scientists in China and India are helping drug companies make huge profits in developing countries.

FUTURE FACT

A recent industry report stated that demand for medicines in China and India will increase by about 10 percent every year until 2015, resulting in a market worth nearly $200 billion.

CHAPTER 1

RISE OF THE PHARMACEUTICAL INDUSTRY

Is the pharmaceutical industry a modern invention? Not at all! The business can trace its roots back to medieval times. The world's first drugstore opened in Baghdad, Iraq, over 1,200 years ago, in A.D. 774.

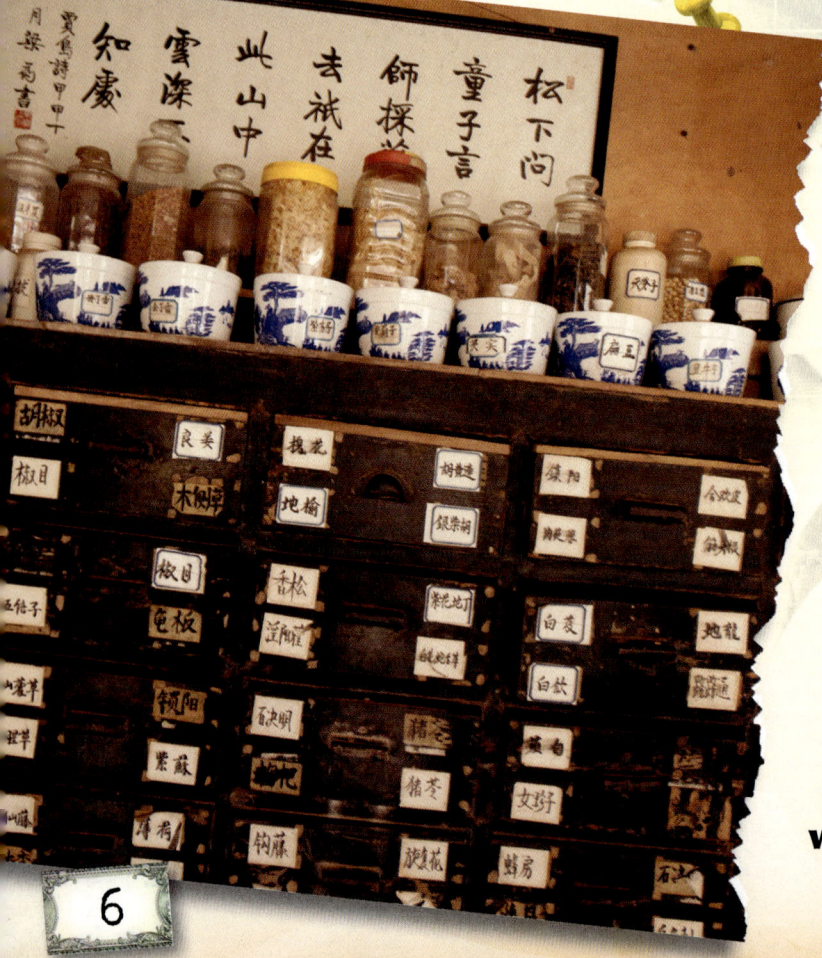

Natural remedies

In the Middle Ages, there were very few tried and tested medicines. Cures offered by drugstores tended to be potions or powders made from natural ingredients. Medieval pharmacists would grind, heat, and mix leaves, plant roots, and fungi to create their natural medicines.

In some countries, such as China, traditional cures that were first developed centuries ago are still popular.

The first medicine factories

The modern pharmaceutical industry only began to take shape in the 19th century. Thanks to an increased understanding of how the human body works, and new scientific methods, drugstores in Europe and America were able to offer proven cures for common illnesses. It wasn't long before some enterprising drugstore owners started opening factories to make their medicines and sell them to other drugstores.

DRUGSTORE ROOTS

Many pharmaceutical corporations can trace their roots back to 19th-century drugstores. Chicago-based Abbott Laboratories first started life in 1885 as a successful drugstore. Its founder, Dr. Wallace C. Abbott, was a local physician who carried out many scientific experiments to find treatments for his patients.

Early drugstores, such as this one in Washington, DC, led to the foundation of the modern pharmaceutical industry.

7

MEDICAL WONDERS

In the early 1900s, many new medicines were discovered, and the industry quickly grew. Companies such as Merck, which perfected a method of producing penicillin on a large scale, began to spend more money on researching new cures. As a result, drugs such as aspirin, paracetamol, and insulin were all introduced.

Safety issues

By the 1950s and 1960s, the pharmaceutical industry was booming. Fueled by great scientific breakthroughs and more accurate methods, a wave of new "wonder drugs" was introduced. Not all of the new drugs were safe, however, and the pharmaceutical industry was rocked by scandals.

Aspirin is now a familiar cure for headaches, but when it was first developed, it was thought of as a medical miracle.

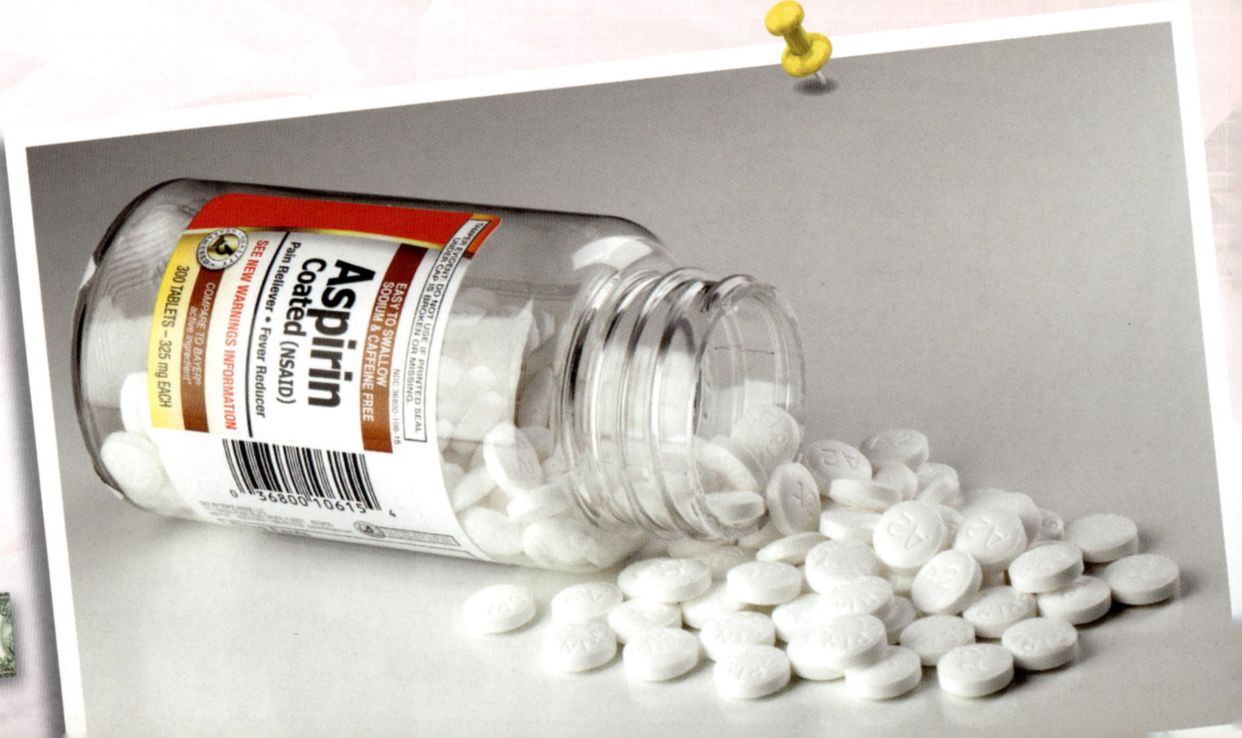

8

DEADLY DRUG

The biggest medical scandal of the 1960s involved the drug Thalidomide, which was given to pregnant women. In 1961, sales were stopped when scientists discovered that thousands of women in Europe who had taken the drug had given birth to babies with severe disabilities. Tragically, many of these babies died.

The work of many brilliant scientists during the 20th century led to the development of a number of life-saving drugs.

Testing is enforced

In 1962, the US government responded to concerns from the public by introducing strict new laws that forced pharmaceutical companies to test drugs more thoroughly. Before new drugs could go on sale, the companies that made them had to prove they were safe. These rules continue to protect the public today.

CHAPTER 2
MAKING MEDICINES

It can take between 10 and 20 years to bring a new drug to market and cost hundreds of millions of dollars. This means that for pharmaceutical corporations, the financial risks are incredibly high. Yet the rewards of success are huge. New wonder drugs can bring in billions of dollars.

A long journey
The process of bringing new drugs to market begins with rigorous scientific research. This is followed by a lengthy period of testing. Drugs that pass the tests—and many do not—may have a patent applied to them, which grants the pharmaceutical corporation exclusive sales rights for a number of years.

Each of the drugs on these shelves could have taken up to 20 years to devise and develop.

The pills being given to this patient may have been made in China or India before being shipped back to the United States.

Manufactured in Asia

Once a new drug has been granted a patent, it can be manufactured. Many medicines developed in the United States are made in factories in China and India, where production costs are far lower. The drugs are then shipped back to the United States, where the process of selling them to health maintenance organizations (HMOs), hospitals, and drugstores begins.

FUTURE FACT

In 2006, annual spending on drugs and medicines in the United States topped $250 billion for the first time. By 2023, industry experts predict that annual sales will have reached a staggering $263 billion.

RESEARCH AND DEVELOPMENT

All around the world, scientists in laboratories are busy working on research to find new drugs and medicines. Many are employed by universities and colleges. Others work directly for pharmaceutical companies.

Investing in research
One area of research that pharmaceutical companies invest in heavily is dangerous diseases. They hope that their scientists will be able to identify new chemical compounds that have the potential to fight, control, or cure these illnesses.

The research of brilliant American scientist John Craig Venter has been the basis of many important medical discoveries.

It can take years of work in laboratories such as this one to create a new drug.

12

Drug discovery

Scientists may spend years trying thousands of different chemical combinations before they find a formula for a successful drug. Only one in 25 successful formulas for medicines will go on to be tested on humans, and by this point, the pharmaceutical company will already have spent many millions of dollars.

STEM CELL RESEARCH

Pharmaceutical companies are spending many millions of dollars on stem cell research. This involves cloning cells from an existing human body and altering the cells to help cure a particular illness.

CLINICAL TRIALS

Once a new drug has been discovered, it must next be tested.
First, "test tube studies" are conducted in the laboratory, where scientists can carefully monitor just how the drug affects human body cells. If the results are positive, the drug may then be tested on animals and then on humans.

Testing drugs on humans
Tests in which drugs are tried out on humans for the first time are called clinical trials. Before these tests can take place, permission must be sought from the US Food and Drug Administration (FDA), the government agency that oversees the pharmaceutical industry.

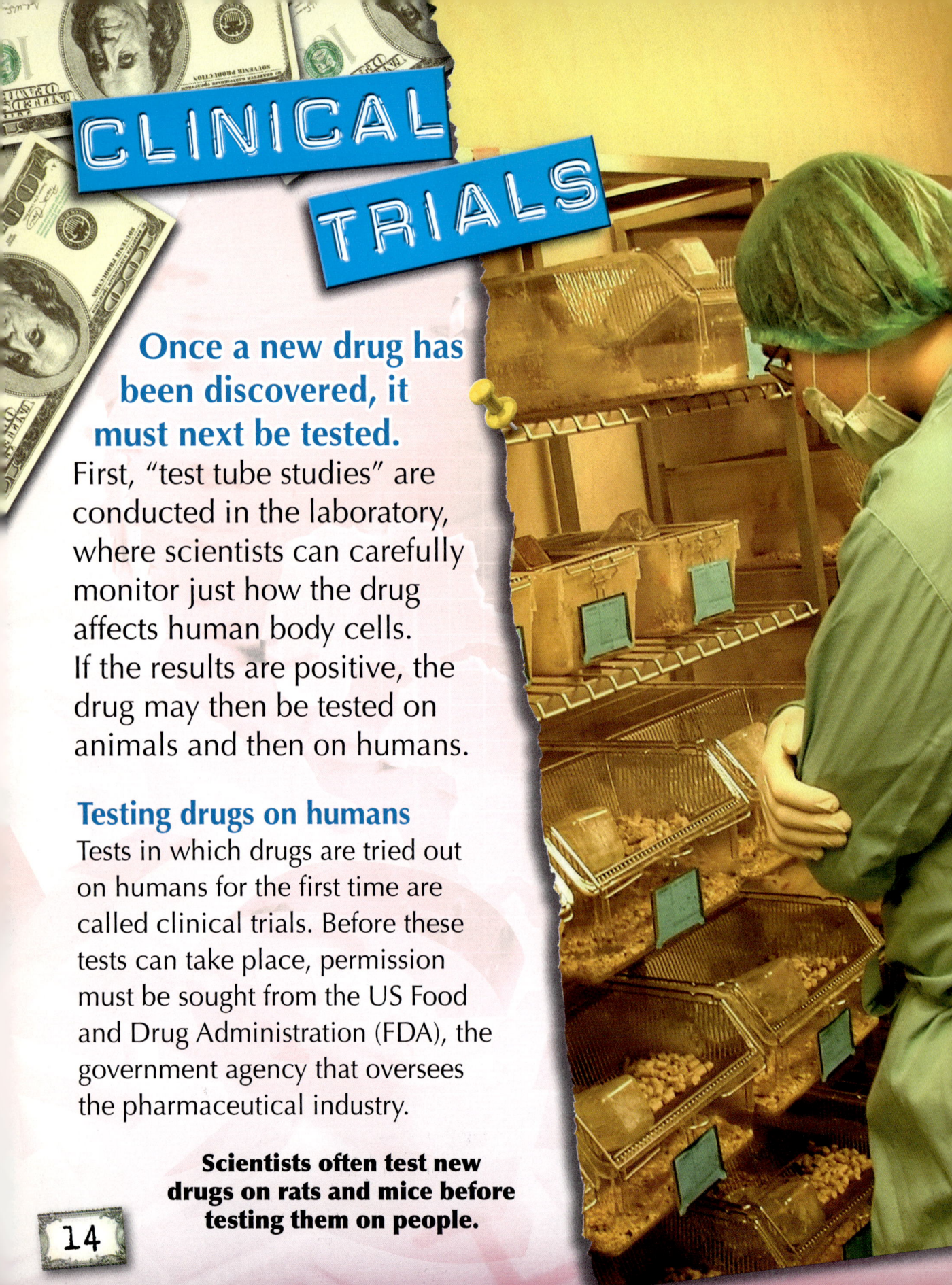

Scientists often test new drugs on rats and mice before testing them on people.

SEEDING TRIALS

In 2001, 12 leading medical magazines all ran an article accusing pharmaceutical companies of using "seeding trials" to sell their products. This means the companies paid doctors to give their new drugs to patients. Because they were being paid, the doctors were rarely critical of the medicines, even when they should have been.

Treating real illnesses

Clinical trials can continue for some time—often for a number of years—and involve several studies in different countries. Usually, the drug will be given to people who have the illness that the drug is designed to treat. Experts are asked to watch the trials and report on whether the new drug works.

Physicians carefully monitor children who take part in clinical trials to make sure that new drugs are safe.

PATENT PENDING

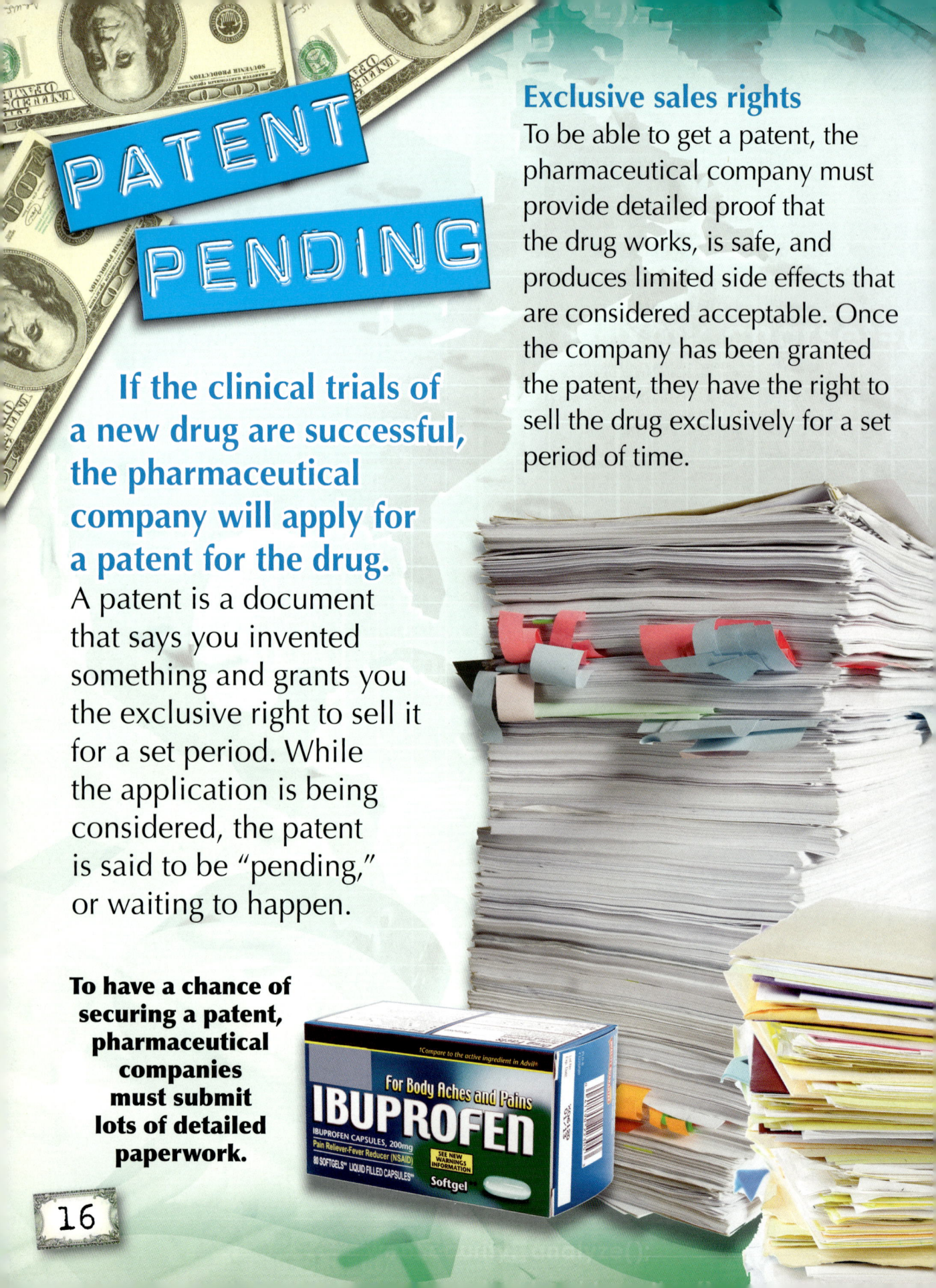

If the clinical trials of a new drug are successful, the pharmaceutical company will apply for a patent for the drug. A patent is a document that says you invented something and grants you the exclusive right to sell it for a set period. While the application is being considered, the patent is said to be "pending," or waiting to happen.

Exclusive sales rights

To be able to get a patent, the pharmaceutical company must provide detailed proof that the drug works, is safe, and produces limited side effects that are considered acceptable. Once the company has been granted the patent, they have the right to sell the drug exclusively for a set period of time.

To have a chance of securing a patent, pharmaceutical companies must submit lots of detailed paperwork.

16

THE COST OF PATENTS

Pharmaceutical companies develop many new drugs at the same time, but only a small number of them are granted a patent. Each successful drug patent costs the pharmaceutical company about $1.3 billion.

Hard to get

In the United States, the FDA grants patents for all new drugs. Its Center for Drug Evaluation and Research oversees the New Drug Application (NDA) process. In 2010, they approved just 21 new drugs for use. This was a tiny portion of the applications received.

It takes years of research and development before a company can apply for a patent for a new drug.

MARKETING MEDICINES

Sales of new wonder drugs need to be huge to cover the billions of dollars spent on research and development. Pharmaceutical companies spend huge amounts of money on marketing to boost their sales. They may even spend twice the amount they spent on research.

What is marketing?

Marketing is the process of making people aware of a product so that they will buy it. Pharmaceutical companies use a number of different marketing methods to try driving up sales. They place ads on TV and in magazines, for example, and give away free samples.

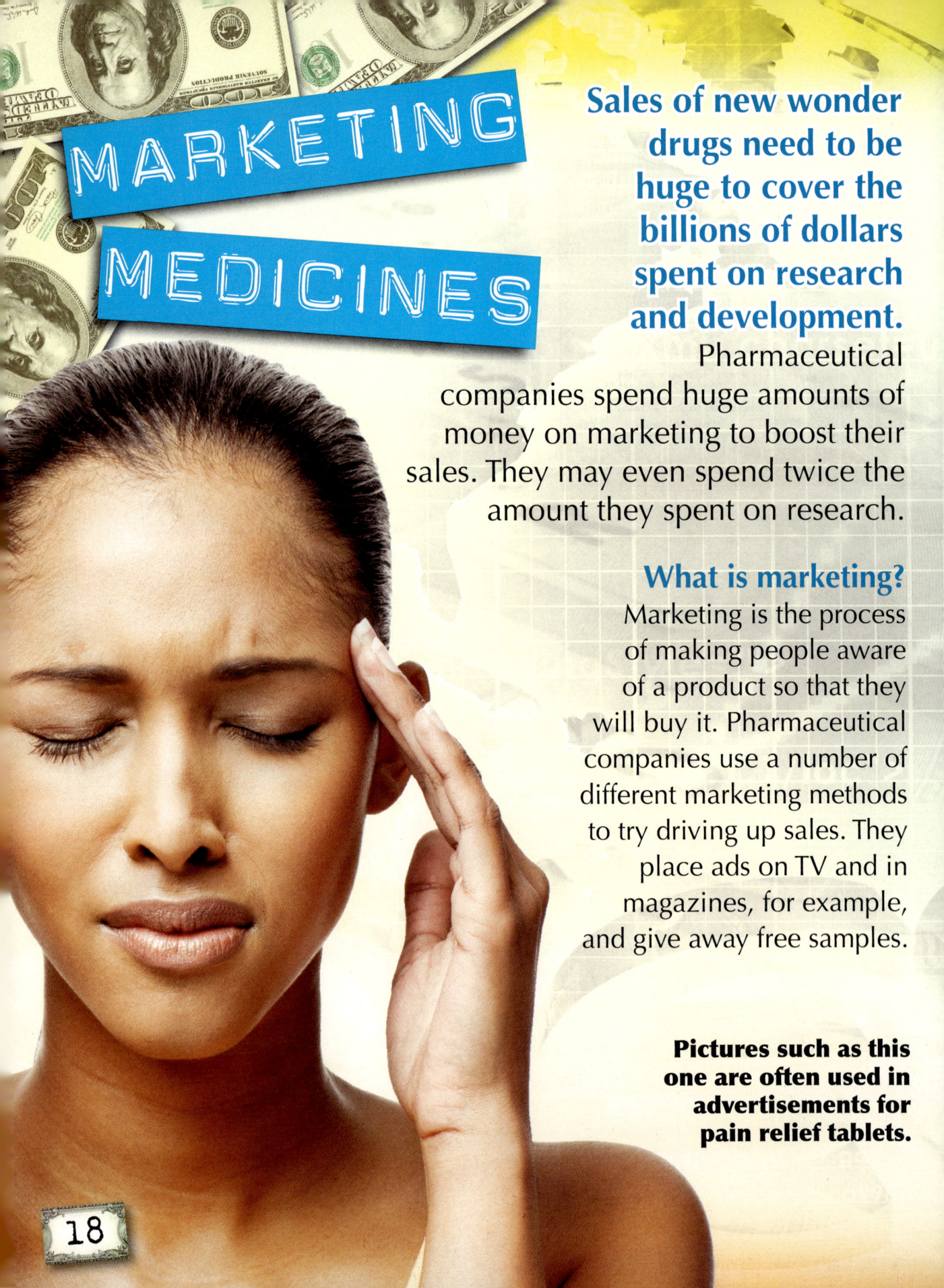

Pictures such as this one are often used in advertisements for pain relief tablets.

The role of drug reps

Most marketing of new drugs is directed at doctors and hospital administrators, because these are the people who have the power to prescribe the drugs and place orders for them. Pharmaceutical corporations pay salespeople called drug reps (short for "representatives") to talk to physicians around the country about the company's medicines.

FUTURE FACT

In the future, the Internet will change the way pharmaceutical companies market their drugs. There are likely to be fewer drug reps and greater use of "e-marketing" aimed directly at HMOs, hospitals, and drugstores.

According to recent research, there are about 61,000 drug reps currently working in the United States.

CHAPTER 3

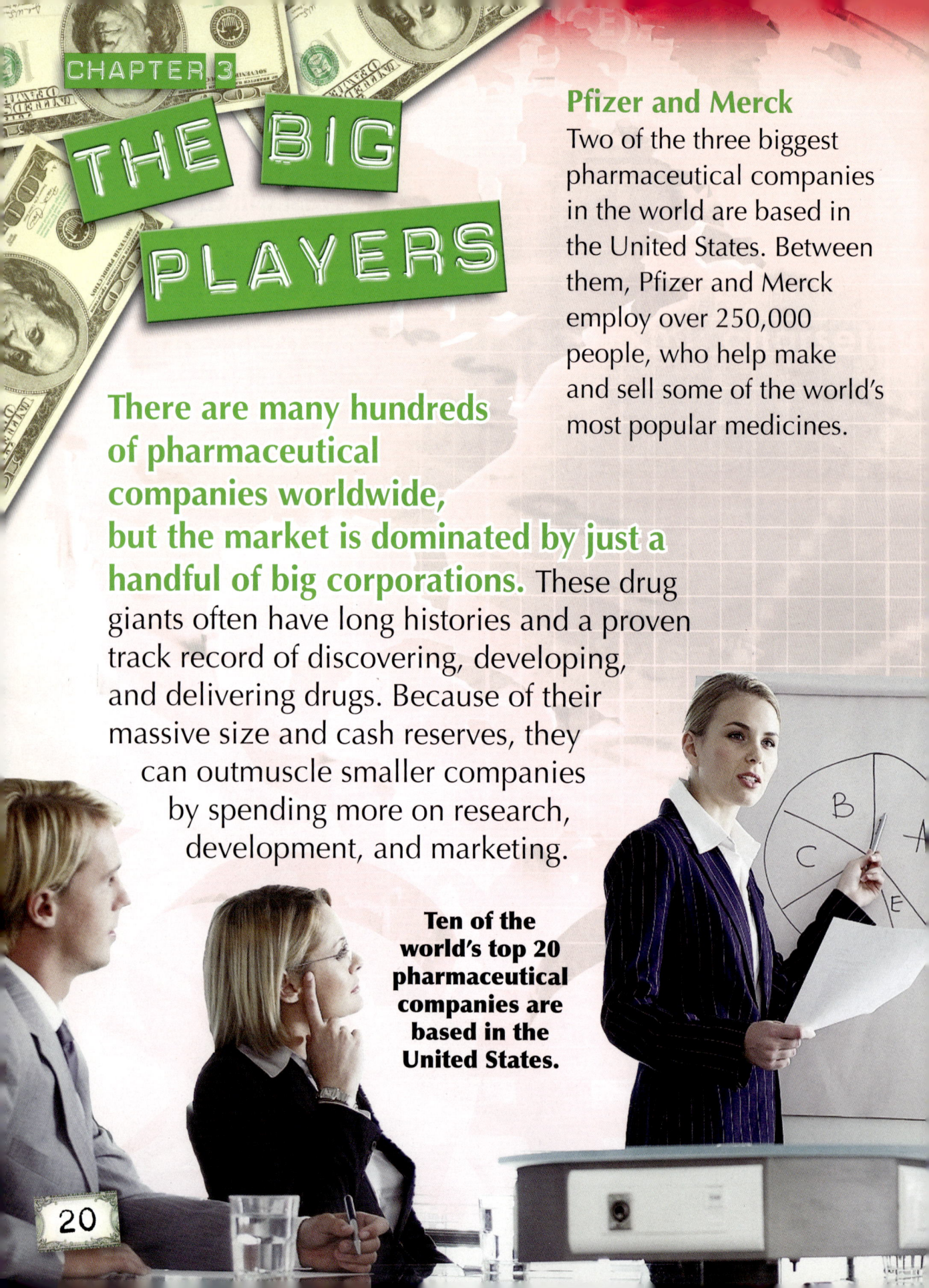

THE BIG PLAYERS

Pfizer and Merck

Two of the three biggest pharmaceutical companies in the world are based in the United States. Between them, Pfizer and Merck employ over 250,000 people, who help make and sell some of the world's most popular medicines.

There are many hundreds of pharmaceutical companies worldwide, but the market is dominated by just a handful of big corporations. These drug giants often have long histories and a proven track record of discovering, developing, and delivering drugs. Because of their massive size and cash reserves, they can outmuscle smaller companies by spending more on research, development, and marketing.

Ten of the world's top 20 pharmaceutical companies are based in the United States.

Tough competition

Corporations such as Pfizer and Merck owe some of their size and success to buying up smaller pharmaceutical companies. In order to compete with these giants, other medical companies around the world have joined forces. GlaxoSmithKline, for example, came about after two huge corporations, GlaxoWellcome and SmithKline Beecham, merged in 2000.

FUTURE FACT

Over the last 10 years, the number of companies making drugs has fallen. This trend is likely to continue in the future as leading corporations buy up or merge with smaller companies.

German pharmaceutical company Bayer made profits of over $1.3 billion in 2010.

RISKY BUSINESS

The pharmaceutical industry is seeing record sales and soaring profits. Yet the business remains a risky one. Bad decisions or poor research can lead to billions of dollars being wasted. For pharmaceutical corporations, the difference between success and failure can be enormous.

Limiting the risk

As we have seen, it takes a lot of time and money to bring a new drug to market. Although pharmaceutical companies try to protect themselves against making the wrong choices by researching and testing many new drugs at once, there are no guarantees that any of their drugs will be approved. A run of failures can harm a company's share price and future growth.

How well a pharmaceutical company is doing will be reflected in its share price. A higher share price means bigger profits.

Pharmaceutical companies must sell new drugs in large quantities to cover the cost of developing them.

THE COST OF FAILURE

In March 2008, British pharmaceutical giant AstraZeneca saw its share price tumble after five different new drugs, including stroke and lung cancer treatments, failed to get past the trial stage. As a result, the company was worth less than a quarter of what it had been a year earlier. Since then, share prices have recovered.

A competitive market

Even if a new drug does make it to market, it must sell in huge numbers. Because drugs are often patented before trial, companies only have five to seven years to maximize sales before competitors are allowed to make their own versions (known as "generic drugs"). Poor sales could lose the company hundreds of millions of dollars.

BILLION-DOLLAR BUSINESSES

Sometimes a pharmaceutical company strikes gold! It develops a wonder drug that sells in vast numbers around the world and makes the company a huge profit. The money it makes from sales of the drug far outweighs the amount it spent on researching, developing, and marketing the drug.

The success of Prozac

American corporation Eli Lilly and Company struck gold when it launched a drug called Prozac in 1987. Prozac was heralded as a brilliant new treatment for depression. In its first year alone, Prozac made Eli Lilly over $350 million. By the time its exclusive patent ran out in 2001, Prozac sales had topped $4 billion.

Stem cells, seen above through a powerful microscope, are the basis for some amazing new cures.

CANCER CURE?

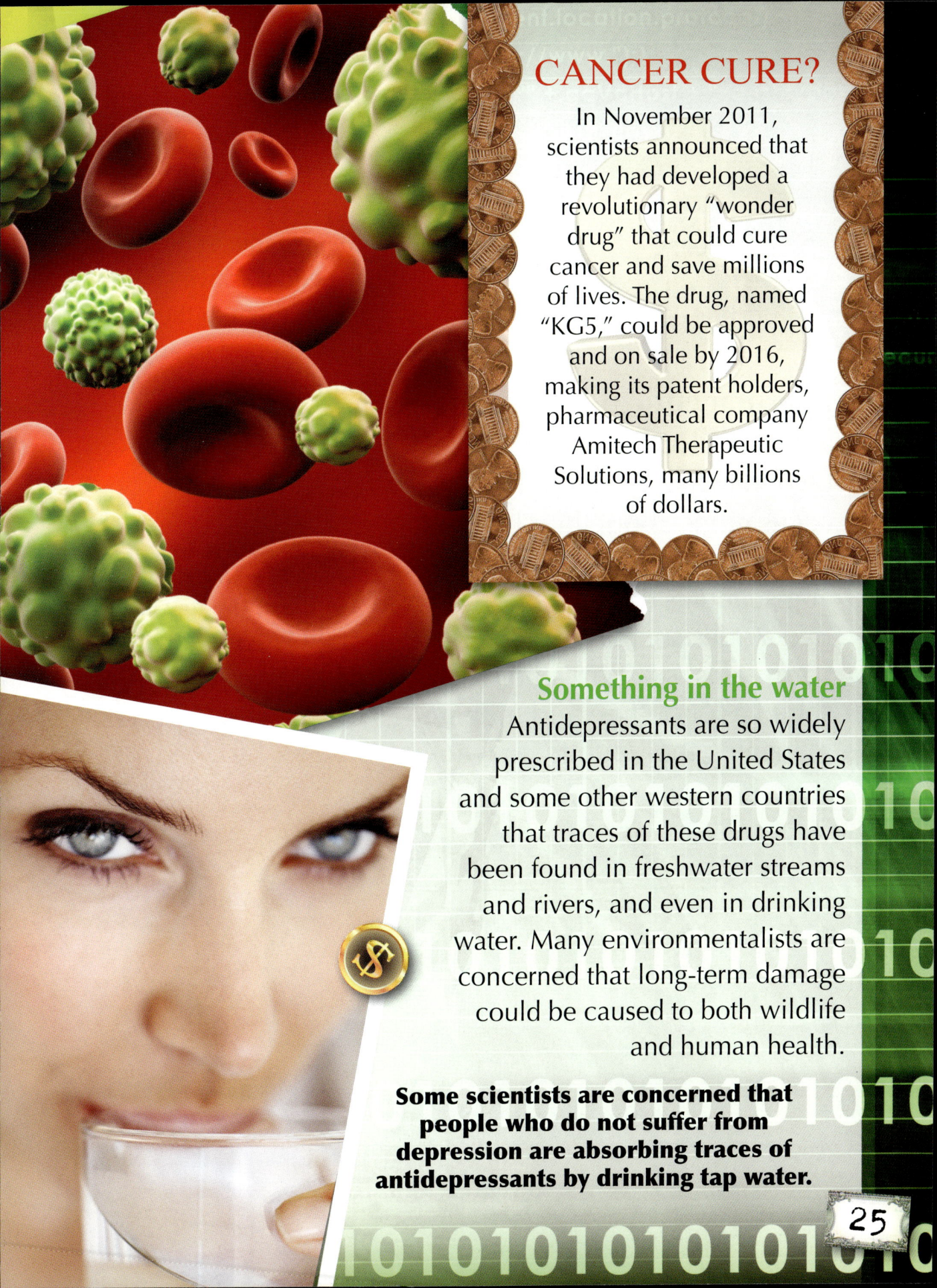

In November 2011, scientists announced that they had developed a revolutionary "wonder drug" that could cure cancer and save millions of lives. The drug, named "KG5," could be approved and on sale by 2016, making its patent holders, pharmaceutical company Amitech Therapeutic Solutions, many billions of dollars.

Something in the water

Antidepressants are so widely prescribed in the United States and some other western countries that traces of these drugs have been found in freshwater streams and rivers, and even in drinking water. Many environmentalists are concerned that long-term damage could be caused to both wildlife and human health.

Some scientists are concerned that people who do not suffer from depression are absorbing traces of antidepressants by drinking tap water.

MANAGING THE IMAGE

Pharmaceutical corporations are not always well liked. Over the years, they've battled accusations about their business practices, the costs of medicines, and scandals over failed drugs. Bad stories such as these can harm sales, so companies spend a lot of time and money managing their public image.

Paying for good publicity
Many pharmaceutical companies pay public relations (PR) or media management companies to send positive stories about them to the media and respond to any bad publicity. They regularly spend hundreds of thousands of dollars each year on PR.

When new drugs given to pregnant women are shown to harm the development of unborn babies, the pharmaceutical industry must react quickly to prevent bad press.

26

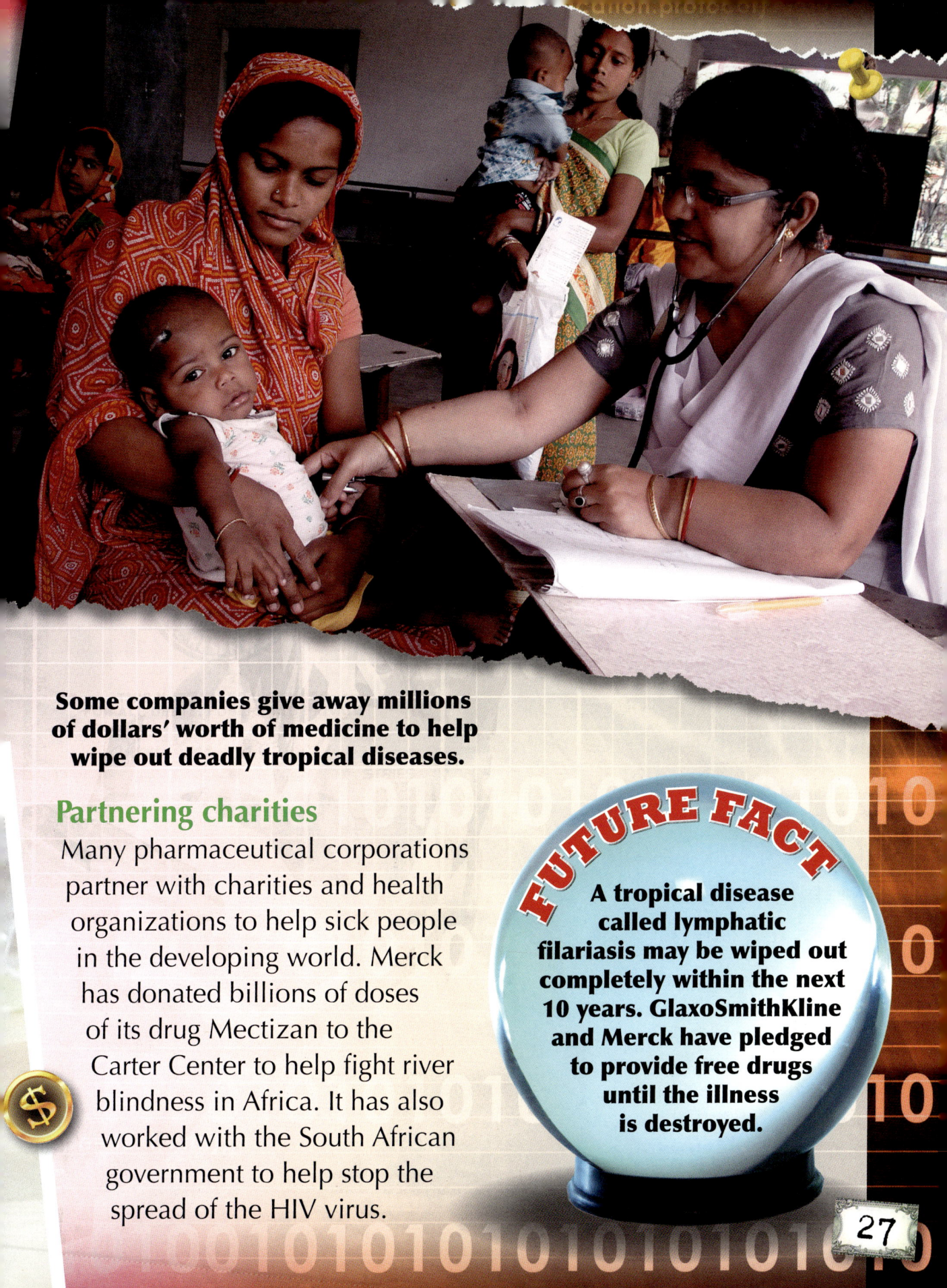

Some companies give away millions of dollars' worth of medicine to help wipe out deadly tropical diseases.

Partnering charities

Many pharmaceutical corporations partner with charities and health organizations to help sick people in the developing world. Merck has donated billions of doses of its drug Mectizan to the Carter Center to help fight river blindness in Africa. It has also worked with the South African government to help stop the spread of the HIV virus.

FUTURE FACT

A tropical disease called lymphatic filariasis may be wiped out completely within the next 10 years. GlaxoSmithKline and Merck have pledged to provide free drugs until the illness is destroyed.

27

CHAPTER 4

CONTROVERSIES AND CHALLENGES

Pharmaceutical companies are rarely out of the news. As if running some of the world's biggest corporations wasn't difficult enough, the bosses of pharmaceutical companies often have to deal with big challenges and global controversies. With the health of sick people on the line, the stakes are often incredibly high.

Decisions made by pharmaceutical companies can affect the lives of millions of sick people around the world.

Bad news

Sometimes pharmaceutical companies must admit that people have become sick after taking new medicines. This can happen as a result of mistakes made by people within the pharmaceutical industry. Another challenge they face is having to argue with national governments about the cost of medicines. They constantly have to balance the goal of making money against the need to keep the world healthy.

In 2011, one pharmaceutical company had to take a popular drug off the market following a health scare.

Is the price fair?

Giant pharmaceutical corporations develop and sell medicines in order to make money, but many people who need their drugs can't afford to buy them. Like a lot of other controversies and challenges that the pharmaceutical industry faces every year, it's a problem that refuses to go away.

DRUG PANIC

In August 2011, the pharmaceutical company Reckitt Benkhiser was forced to recall thousands of packets of a pain relief drug called Nurofen Plus. Several batches sent to drugstores in London, England, were found to contain a powerful drug used in the treatment of mental health illnesses.

29

FEAR TACTICS?

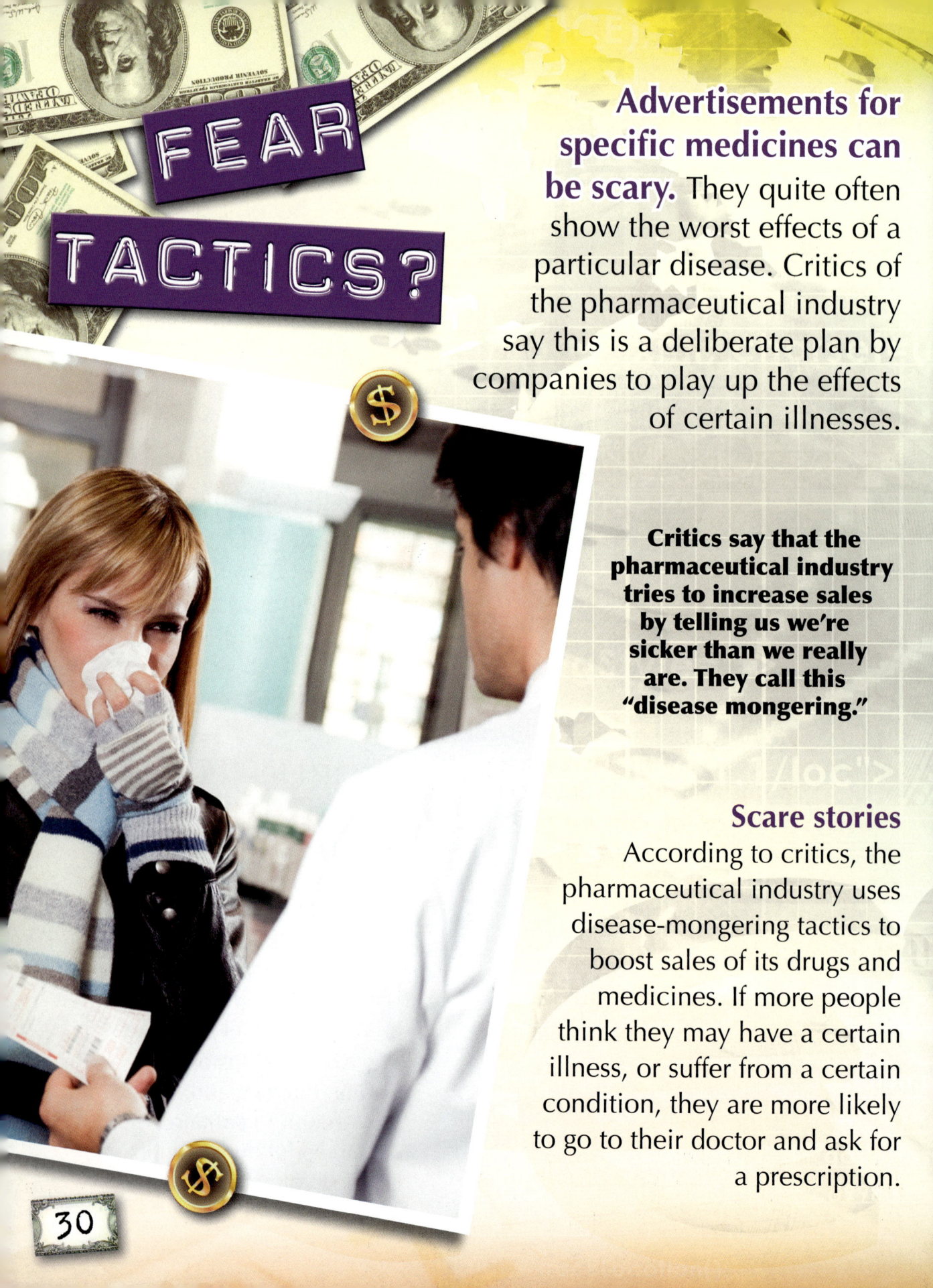

Advertisements for specific medicines can be scary. They quite often show the worst effects of a particular disease. Critics of the pharmaceutical industry say this is a deliberate plan by companies to play up the effects of certain illnesses.

Critics say that the pharmaceutical industry tries to increase sales by telling us we're sicker than we really are. They call this "disease mongering."

Scare stories

According to critics, the pharmaceutical industry uses disease-mongering tactics to boost sales of its drugs and medicines. If more people think they may have a certain illness, or suffer from a certain condition, they are more likely to go to their doctor and ask for a prescription.

Testing people for illnesses such as diabetes can help drive sales of drugs.

The case for the defense

The pharmaceutical industry denies that it uses disease-mongering tactics. Companies say they offer information to the public about illnesses and the drugs that could help fight or cure them. They also point out that they have no control over what medicines doctors actually prescribe for their patients.

MARKETING MISHAP

US pharmaceutical giant Eli Lilly was fined a record $515 million and forced to pay out billions of dollars in compensation after being found guilty of playing down the side effects of the mental health drug Zyprexa. Thousands of people who took the drug put on weight and developed diabetes.

31

THE COST OF ERROR

Most new drugs developed and sold by pharmaceutical companies are safe. A small number, however, prove to have unpredicted side effects. On occasion, drugs that may help treat one illness are found to cause other health problems. When this happens, it can cost pharmaceutical corporations billions of dollars.

If people get sick after taking a drug, it's bad news for the pharmaceutical industry.

Initial success ...

When Merck launched Vioxx in 1999, it was marketed as a wonder drug that would relieve the pain of many millions of arthritis sufferers worldwide. It was a huge success, and by 2003, sales had risen to over $2.5 billion a year.

SIDE EFFECTS

Some scientists have suggested links between certain antidepressants and the suicidal thoughts of young people taking those drugs. The pharmaceutical companies deny a link. They are fighting a number of court cases brought by the parents of teenagers.

Vioxx was one of Merck's biggest-selling drugs until it was withdrawn.

Withdrawn from sale

In 2004, Merck took the dramatic decision to withdraw Vioxx from sale because of safety concerns. The FDA estimated that Vioxx had caused between 88,000 and 139,000 heart attacks in five years. Since then, Merck has paid out hundreds of millions of dollars in compensation to former users. Eventually, the total cost to the company could be $5 billion.

COZY RELATIONSHIPS

Researchers, doctors, and pharmaceutical companies have always had a close relationship. Some people think it is too close and that the pharmaceutical industry has too much power over health and science professionals.

Drug companies have been criticized for offering doctors free gifts, such as skiing vacations.

Tied by money

Critics say that some scientists feel under pressure to deliver the results that pharmaceutical companies want, because it is these companies who pay their wages. They allege that some scientists will design tests that only deliver results that show new drugs in a favorable light.

Critics say scientific research used by the pharmaceutical industry is flawed.

New guidelines

In recent years, the relationship between drug reps and doctors has been in the spotlight. In the past, it wasn't uncommon for drug reps to offer gifts as incentives to doctors in order to get them to buy their medicines. Following criticism, the pharmaceutical industry introduced new guidelines in 2009 to end these practices.

NO FREE GIFTS

The close relationship between drug reps and doctors isn't just an issue in the United States. In the United Kingdom, where citizens enjoy free health care, rules have been introduced to try to put an end to the free gifts given by pharmaceutical companies to doctors.

GLOBAL ISSUES

Around the world, and particularly in Africa, millions of people suffer from a potentially deadly virus called HIV. Plenty of cutting-edge drug treatments exist to fight the virus, but because pharmaceutical companies own the patents, they can charge top prices.

It is much easier for people in the West to get the drugs they need to combat HIV.

DANGEROUS DRUG TRIALS

The pharmaceutical company Pfizer was accused of testing a new, unproven drug on 100 children in Nigeria in 1996 without their permission. Several children died, and others became sick. In 2009, Pfizer agreed to pay out $75 million in compensation to the victims.

Making a stand

It costs an estimated $10,000 per person, per year to treat HIV in South Africa, where hundreds of thousands of people have the virus. In 2001 the South African government said it could not afford to pay such high prices. It passed a law allowing the country to bypass the drug companies and make its own copycat "generic" drugs for a fraction of the price.

In developing countries, children with HIV now have a chance to live longer thanks to donated drugs.

The industry backs down

The pharmaceutical companies decided to sue the South African government. However, in the face of mounting pressure from campaigners, they eventually backed down. Now they work with the World Health Organization to offer cheap or free HIV drugs in developing countries.

CHAPTER 5

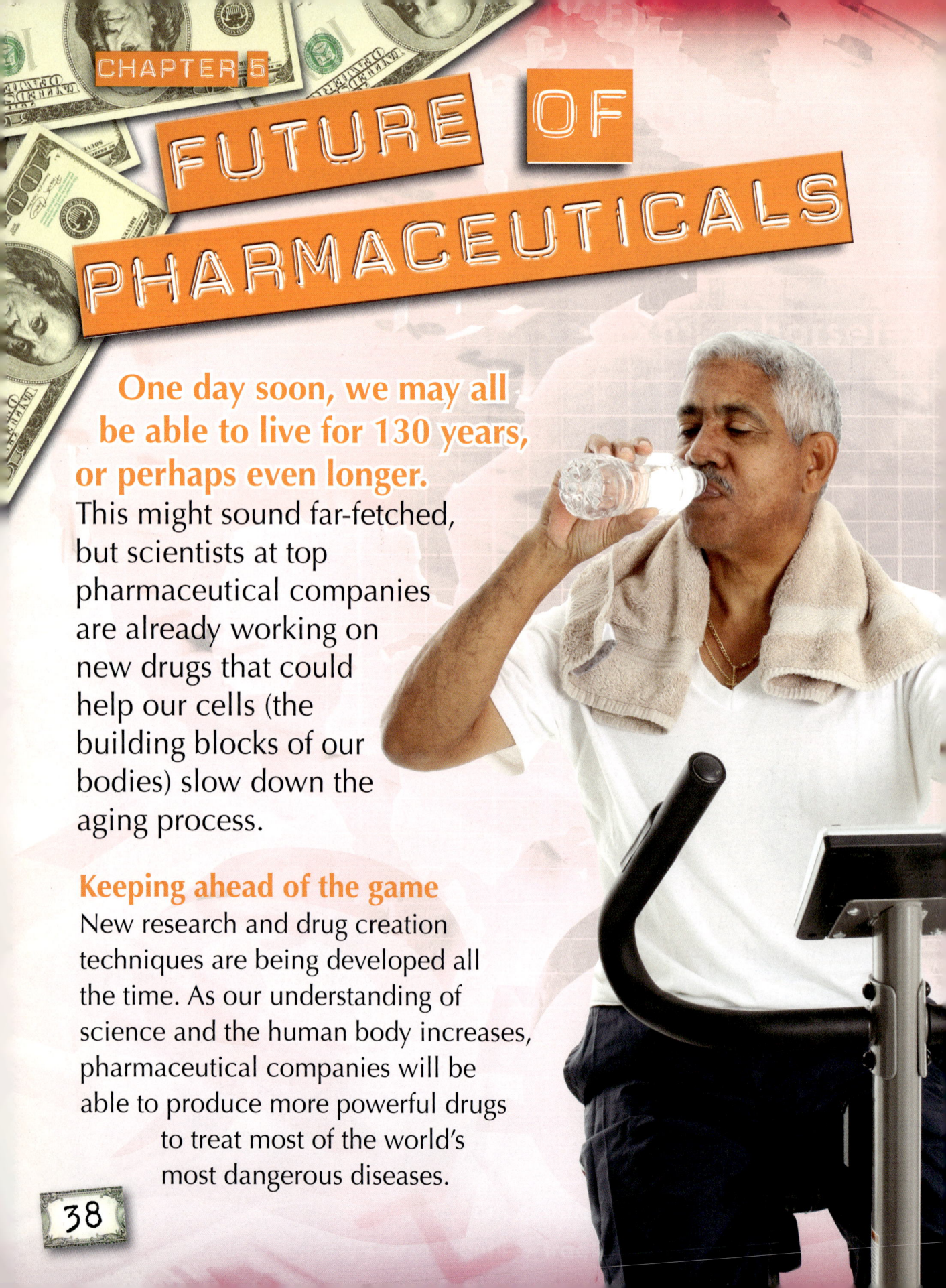

FUTURE OF PHARMACEUTICALS

One day soon, we may all be able to live for 130 years, or perhaps even longer. This might sound far-fetched, but scientists at top pharmaceutical companies are already working on new drugs that could help our cells (the building blocks of our bodies) slow down the aging process.

Keeping ahead of the game

New research and drug creation techniques are being developed all the time. As our understanding of science and the human body increases, pharmaceutical companies will be able to produce more powerful drugs to treat most of the world's most dangerous diseases.

Thanks to medical science, many Americans now live longer, healthier lives.

Stem cells such as this one are helping scientists repair our bodies in amazing new ways.

Challenges ahead

The pharmaceutical industry still has challenges to face, though. The debate over the balance between keeping the world healthy and maximizing company profits will continue, and the industry's business practices will be scrutinized more than ever.

FUTURE FACTS

Doctors can now repair body parts using cells created in a laboratory. In the future, this kind of stem cell treatment is likely to get more advanced. Doctors may one day be able to grow organs such as the heart and kidneys in a laboratory.

AGE OF THE INTERNET

Since the Internet boom of the 1990s, the World Wide Web has changed the way most companies do business. The pharmaceutical industry was quick to see that, by using the Internet, it could get its message across directly to potential customers.

Online selling

As well as having their own corporate websites with information about their businesses, pharmaceutical companies also have sites for each of their branded medicines. These websites are designed not only to provide advice and safety information, but also to sell medications to drugstores, doctors, and ordinary people.

Many people now buy their medicines through online pharmacy stores.

40

Plugging products

Websites for "over-the-counter medicines" (ones that you can buy from a drugstore without a prescription) either offer links to online pharmacies or talk up the benefits of the products to encourage you to buy them. For nonprescription products, the web has proved to be a very useful marketing tool.

FDA CLAMPDOWN

In 2009, the FDA clamped down on misleading Internet ads from pharmaceutical companies. It sent warning letters to 14 of the world's biggest drug corporations.

Many people now prefer to buy medicines online using the Internet.

41

FIGHTING ILLEGAL MEDICINES

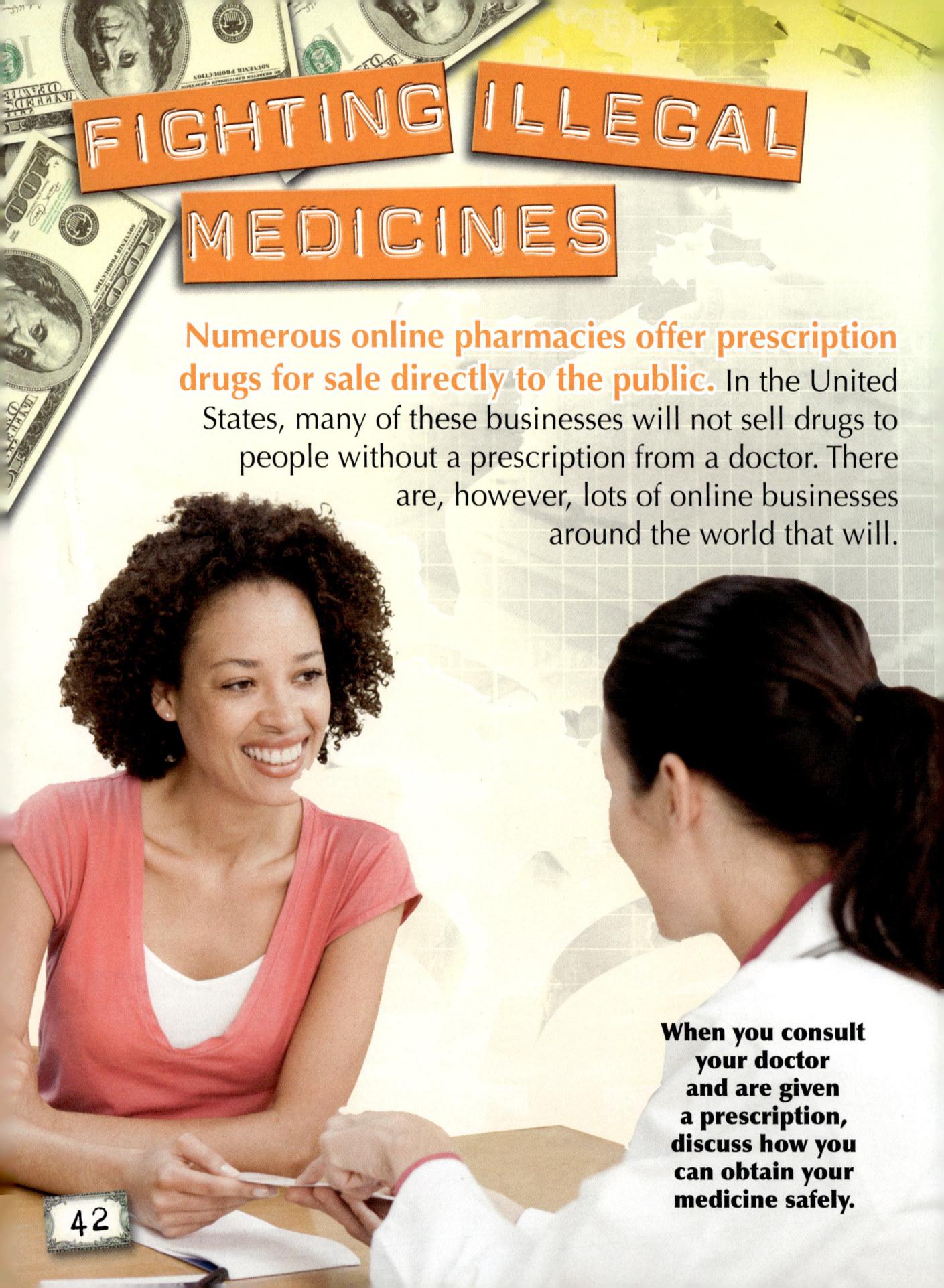

Numerous online pharmacies offer prescription drugs for sale directly to the public. In the United States, many of these businesses will not sell drugs to people without a prescription from a doctor. There are, however, lots of online businesses around the world that will.

When you consult your doctor and are given a prescription, discuss how you can obtain your medicine safely.

Cheap drugs

Outside of the United States, many online pharmacies give no guarantee that the drugs they sell are safe. Buying from them is illegal, and shoppers who are caught can be sent to jail. People continue to take the risk, however, because medications bought from online pharmacies are usually much cheaper.

Buying online is risky because you cannot really know what you are purchasing.

LIFESTYLE DRUGS

Many people use online pharmacies to buy so-called lifestyle drugs, which treat nonthreatening conditions such as baldness or spots. The market for these drugs is very lucrative for the pharmaceutical industry.

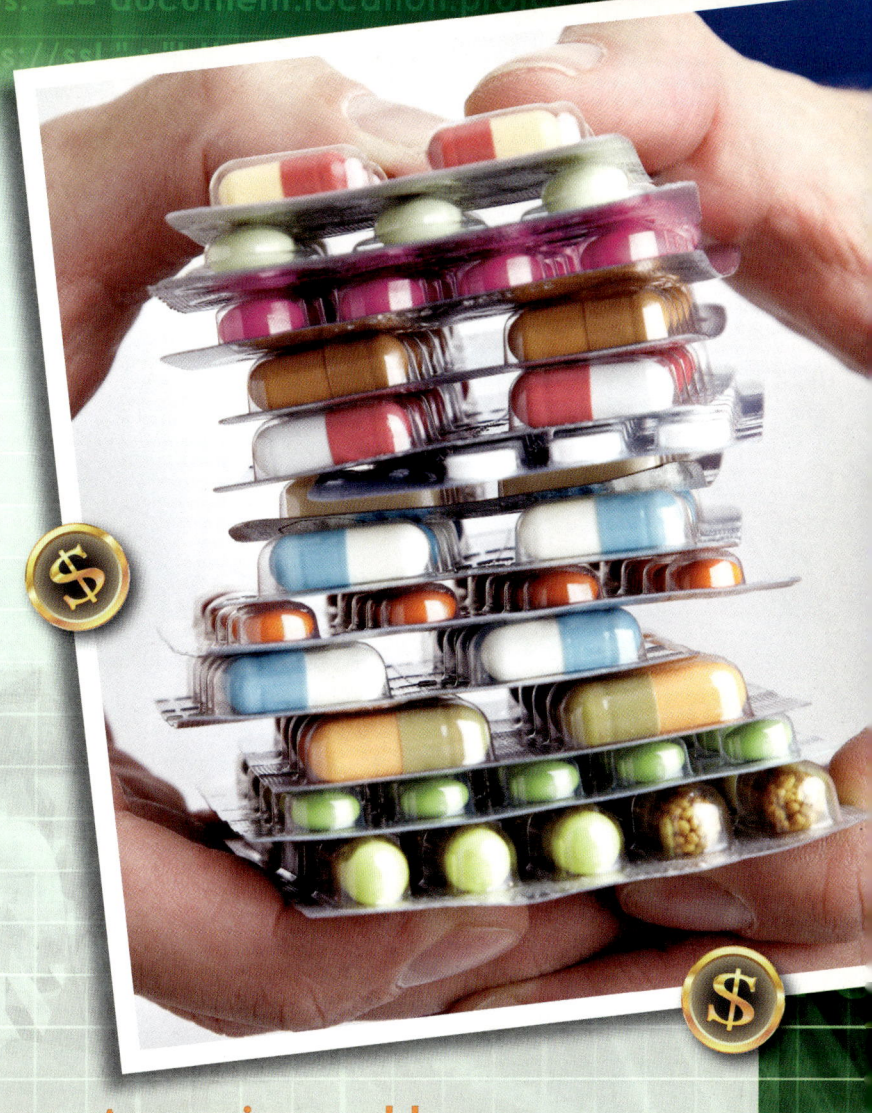

A growing problem

Americans spend over $1 billion a year illegally buying drugs from foreign online pharmacies. While this is a relatively small amount compared to total online drug sales of $75 billion a year, it represents a significant loss of potential profits for pharmaceutical companies. With around 4,700 unregistered online pharmacies in the United States alone, it is a growing problem for the industry.

LIVING FOREVER

In 1911, the average life expectancy of an American man was 47 years, but in 2011, it was nearly 80! These amazing statistics show just how big a difference a century of medical and pharmaceutical advances have made to the way we live our lives. We're now living much longer. By 2050, the average life expectancy of an American woman could be close to 100 years.

Drug use set to increase

Longer life expectancy is great news for the pharmaceutical industry. As people get older, they need more drugs and medications to keep them healthy. If more of us live longer, demand for key drugs will rocket. For the pharmaceutical industry, this means ever-increasing future sales.

Pharmaceutical industry profits are expected to rise for years to come.

Amazing new drugs are helping people to live longer, healthier, more active lives.

FUTURE FACT

The world's population currently stands at about 7 billion. According to United Nations projections, by 2050, it could top 10 billion. That's a lot more people for the pharmaceutical industry to keep healthy!

New drugs offer hope

Over the next 50 years, our understanding of how to treat deadly diseases and viruses will increase significantly. Pharmaceutical companies will develop new wonder drugs to fight cancer, HIV, and other terrible illnesses. These drugs will be sold at premium prices, allowing pharmaceutical companies to announce record profits for years to come.

GLOSSARY

billion a thousand million, or 1,000,000,000

branded medicines drugs sold to the public and health professionals using a "trade name," for example, Prozac

cash reserves money that companies have stored in a bank for future use

cloning producing an accurate copy of something, such as body cells

compensation money paid to a person by a company if the person has suffered because of something the company has done

controversies major disputes, usually held in public

depression a disease of the mind that makes you sad

disabilities permanent problems with the mind or body, such as legs that don't work or severe mental illness

e-marketing electronic marketing done using email or the Internet

exclusive restricted to one person or company

generic drugs cheap copies of drugs no longer protected by a patent

incentives gifts given to someone to encourage them to do something specific

laboratories the rooms in which scientists carry out research and experiments

mental health drug a medicine used to treat a disease of the mind

mental health illnesses diseases of the mind

patent a legal document that proves you are the inventor of a product and makes it illegal for other people to copy it

patient anyone who sees a doctor for advice when they are ill

pharmacy another word for drugstore

physician another word for doctor

premium prices sum added to the ordinary price of a good, making it more expensive

prescription drugs drugs that can be obtained only with a written order from a doctor

profits money that a business makes on top of the money it has spent on buying or producing something

public relations the business of managing the public image of a company or individual

research finding out more about something in order to understand it better

share price the price for which part of a company can be bought or sold. If the price is high, the company is doing well.

side effects illnesses or physical conditions that result from taking a particular medicine

successful formulas combinations of chemicals proven to work as medicines

sue to take somebody to court over something they've said or done

suicidal thoughts thinking about killing yourself

FOR MORE INFORMATION

BOOKS

Coad, John. *Finding Better Medicines* (Why Science Matters). Chicago, IL: Heinemann-Raintree, 2008.

Rooney, Anne. *Health and Medicines: The Impact of Science and Technology*. New York, NY: Gareth Stevens Publishing, 2009.

Rosinsky, Natalie Myra. *The Story of Pharmaceuticals: How They Changed the World*. Mankato, MN: Compass Point Books, 2010.

Spilsbury, Richard. *Pharmaceutical Industry: A Closer Look* (Global Industries). New York, NY: Rosen Central, 2010.

WEBSITES

Find out more about the pharmaceutical industry and your health at:

www.fda.gov

www.merck.com/index.html

www.kidshealth.org/teen/index.jsp?tracking=T_Home

teens.webmd.com/default.htm

Publisher's note to educators and parents: Our editors have carefully reviewed these websites to ensure that they are suitable for students. Many websites change frequently, however, and we cannot guarantee that a site's future contents will continue to meet our high standards of quality and educational value. Be advised that students should be closely supervised whenever they access the Internet.

INDEX

Abbott Laboratories 7
Africa 27, 36, 37
Amitech Therapeutic Solutions 25
Asia 11
AstraZeneca 23

Bayer 21
branded medicines 40

China 5, 6, 11
clinical trials 14, 15, 16
cloning 13
compensation 31, 33, 37

disease mongering 30, 31
diseases 12, 27, 30, 36, 37, 38, 45
drug discovery 13
drug reps 19, 35
drugstores 4, 6, 7, 11, 19, 29, 40, 41

Eli Lilly and Company 24, 31
e-marketing 19

generic drugs 23, 37, 46
GlaxoSmithKline 21, 27

health maintenance organizations (HMOs) 11, 19
HIV 27, 36, 37, 45

illegal medicines 42, 43
India 5, 11
Internet 19, 40, 41

laboratories 7, 12, 14
life expectancy 44
lifestyle drugs 43

marketing 18, 19, 20, 24, 33, 41
mental health 29, 31
Merck 8, 20, 21, 27, 33

online pharmacies 40, 41, 42, 43
over-the-counter medicines 41

patents 10, 11, 16, 17, 23, 24, 25, 36
Pfizer 4, 20, 21, 37
physician 7, 15, 19
profits 4, 5, 21, 22, 24, 39, 43, 44, 45
Prozac 24
public relations (PR) 26

Reckitt Benkhiser 29
research/researching 8, 10, 12, 13, 17, 18, 20, 22, 24, 35, 38

scandals 8, 9, 26
scientists 5, 9, 12, 13, 14, 25, 33, 35, 38
seeding trials 15
side effects 16, 31, 32, 33
South African government 27, 37
stem cells 13, 24, 39

Thalidomide 9

US Food and Drug Administration (FDA) 14, 17, 33, 41

Vioxx 33

wonder drugs 8, 10, 18, 24, 25, 33, 45
World Health Organization 37